My Canada
NEWFOUNDLAND AND LABRADOR
By Sheila Yazdani

TABLE OF CONTENTS

Newfoundland and Labrador .. 3

Glossary 22

Index 24

A Crabtree Seedlings Book

Crabtree Publishing
crabtreebooks.com

School-to-Home Support for Caregivers and Teachers

This book helps children grow by letting them practice reading. Here are a few guiding questions to help the reader build his or her comprehension skills. Possible answers appear in red.

Before Reading:

- What do I know about Newfoundland and Labrador?
  - *I know that Newfoundland and Labrador is a province.*
  - *I know that Newfoundland and Labrador has a lot of beaches.*

- What do I want to learn about Newfoundland and Labrador?
  - *I want to learn what activities I can do in Newfoundland and Labrador.*
  - *I want to learn what the provincial flag looks like.*

During Reading:

- What have I learned so far?
  - *I have learned that St. John's is the capital of Newfoundland and Labrador.*
  - *I have learned that there are many interesting rocks at the Tablelands.*

- I wonder why…
  - *I wonder why the provincial flower is the pitcher plant.*
  - *I wonder why puffins nest every summer near Cape Bonavista Lighthouse.*

After Reading:

- What did I learn about Newfoundland and Labrador?
  - *I have learned that St. John's is the largest city in Newfoundland and Labrador.*
  - *I have learned that the provincial bird is the Atlantic puffin.*

- Read the book again and look for the glossary words.
  - *I see the word **capital** on page 6, and the word **lighthouse** on page 18. The other glossary words are found on pages 22 and 23.*

Newfoundland and Labrador is made up of the **island** of Newfoundland and the **mainland** area of Labrador.

I live in Trinity. My town is on Newfoundland.

Newfoundland and Labrador is a **province** in eastern Canada. The **capital** is St. John's.

Fun Fact: St. John's is the largest city in Newfoundland and Labrador.

The provincial bird is the Atlantic puffin.

The pitcher plant is the provincial flower.

Fun Fact: Newfoundland and Labrador catches 98,000 metric tons (108,000 tons) of seafood a year.

My provincial flag is blue, red, white, and gold. It has six triangles and an arrow.

I learn about **Viking** history at L'Anse aux Meadows.

Fun Fact: The rocks in the Tablelands are hundreds of millions of years old.

My family goes walking on the East Coast Trail.

I like to have fun exploring at Cape Bonavista **Lighthouse**.

Fun Fact: Every summer, puffins come to nest near Cape Bonavista Lighthouse.

I like to visit the North Atlantic Aviation Museum in Gander. I learn about the history of airplanes and the Gander International Airport.

Glossary

capital (CAP-ih-tuhl): The city or town where the government of a country, state, or province is located

island (IE-lind): Land that is surrounded by water

lighthouse (LIET-hows): A tower with a strong light that is used to guide ships

mainland (MEYN-land): Forming the main part of a region, not including the islands around it

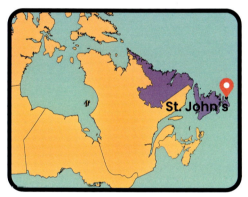

province (PROV-ins): One of the large areas that some countries, such as Canada, are divided into

Viking (VIE-king): A warrior from Scandinavia, an area in northern Europe. Vikings traveled by ship and attacked other countries between the 8th and 11th centuries.

Index

Atlantic puffin 8, 19
Cape Bonavista Lighthouse 18, 19
icebergs 17
seafood 10, 11
St. John's 6, 7
Trinity 5

Written by: Sheila Yazdani
Designed and Illustrated by: Bobbie Houser
Series Development: James Earley
Proofreader: Melissa Boyce
Educational Consultant: Marie Lemke M.Ed.

About the Author

Sheila Yazdani lives in Ontario near Niagara Falls with her dog Daisy. She likes to travel across Canada to learn about its history, people, and landscape. She loves to cook new dishes she learns about. Her favorite treat is Nanaimo bars.

Photographs:
Alamy: Itsik Marom: p. 20
Shutterstock: christopher babcock: cover; CookiesForDevo: p. 3; EB Adventure Photography: p. 4-5, 22-23; Media Guru: p. 6, 22-23; valleyboi63: p. 7; Suwipat Lorsiripaiboon: p. 8; Bill Kennedy: p. 9; Paul Brady Photography: p. 10-11; Mary Anne Love: p. 11; Millenius: p. 12; George Burba: p. 13, 23; EyesTravelling: p. 14-15; Chiyacat: p. 15; jrtwynam: p. 16; ggw: p. 17; Gina Smith: p. 18, 22; FotoRequest: p. 19; George Burba: p. 21

Crabtree Publishing

crabtreebooks.com   800-387-7650
Copyright © 2025 Crabtree Publishing
All rights reserved. No part of this publication may be reproduced, stored in a retrieval system or be transmitted in any form or by any means, electronic, mechanical, photocopying, recording, or otherwise, without the prior written permission of Crabtree Publishing. In Canada: We acknowledge the financial support of the Government of Canada through the Canada Book Fund for our publishing activities.
Printed in Canada/012024/CP20231127

Published in Canada
Crabtree Publishing
616 Welland Avenue
St. Catharines, Ontario
L2M 5V6

Published in the United States
Crabtree Publishing
347 Fifth Avenue
Suite 1402-145
New York, New York, 10016

Library and Archives Canada Cataloguing in Publication
Available at Library and Archives Canada

Library of Congress Cataloging-in-Publication Data
Available at the Library of Congress

Hardcover: 978-1-0398-3855-0
Paperback: 978-1-0398-3940-3
Ebook (pdf): 978-1-0398-4021-8
Epub: 978-1-0398-4093-5